MALCOLM FREDERICK is an actor, author and producer perhaps best known as 'Beastie' on the 1980s television comedy series *No Problem*, and for his roles in the comedy sketch show *Get Up, Stand Up*, which he also produced. With the Carib Theatre Company he has produced *Sweet Inspiration*, a celebration of Caribbean words and music from the 50s and 60s. Malcolm lives in Surrey.

PRODEEPTA DAS was born in Cuttack, in eastern India. Currently a freelance photographer and author, his pictures have been published in over 20 children's titles. In 1991 *Inside India*, which he also wrote, won the Commonwealth Photographers' Award. His previous books for Frances Lincoln are *I is for India, Geeta's Day, We Are Britain, P is for Pakistan, K is for Korea, J is for Jamaica, P is for Poland, B is for Bangladesh* and *Prita Goes to India*. Prodeepta lives in East London.

Kamal Goes to Trinidad

For my parents Cantuell & Norma Frederick, and for my friends
and family in Morvant, Trinidad & Tobago – M.F.

For Hugh Grant and all those who helped me in Trinidad and Tobago – P.D.

Kamal Goes to Trinidad copyright © Frances Lincoln Limited 2008
Text copyright © Malcolm Frederick 2008
Photographs copyright © Prodeepta Das 2008

First published in Great Britain and the USA in 2008 by
Frances Lincoln Children's Books, 4 Torriano Mews,
Torriano Avenue, London NW5 2RZ
www.franceslincoln.com

First paperback edition published in Great Britain in 2010 and in the USA in 2011

A catalogue record for this book is available from the British Library.

ISBN: 978-1-84780-042-8

Set in Minion

Printed in Singapore

1 3 5 7 9 8 6 4 2

Kamal
Goes to
Trinidad

Malcolm Frederick

Photographs by Prodeepta Das

F

FRANCES LINCOLN
CHILDREN'S BOOKS

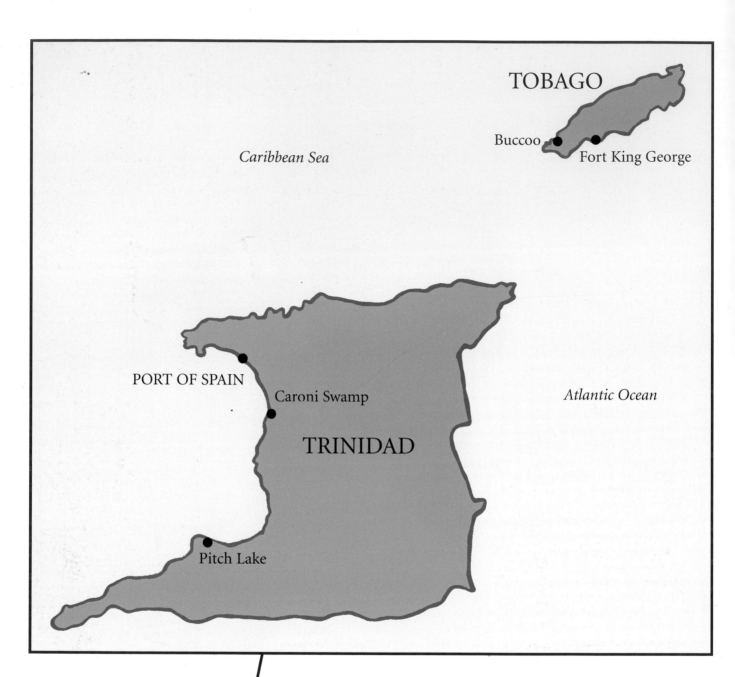

TOBAGO

Caribbean Sea

Buccoo

Fort King George

PORT OF SPAIN

Caroni Swamp

Atlantic Ocean

TRINIDAD

Pitch Lake

U.S.A

South
America

I'm so excited! Today I'm flying to Trinidad and Tobago with my dad and sister Remi. Trinidad and Tobago are islands in the West Indies where my dad and mum were born. Mum isn't coming with us because she's very busy at work. We are going on a big plane and we'll be up in the clouds for 9 hours!

Tobago

When we flew into Tobago, my dad's friends Keith and
Yvonne were waiting for us and took us to their house.

The next morning, as soon as we got up, we explored the garden. It was full of flowers and fruit trees I've never seen before – and an interesting caterpillar.

Yvonne picked us some fruit for breakfast. We had banana, mango, avocado and pineapple – yum yum!

After breakfast we went to the beach. It had palm trees from end to end and soft sand. There were hammocks strung up here and there, with people selling colourful beach wraps. Remi and I went straight into the water. "It's freezing! we shouted, but we soon got used to it.

Then we took a boat ride to the Buccoo Reef. The boat had a glass bottom, so we could see under the water. There were rainbow fish, sea-snakes, anemones, coral, starfish and sting rays.

Later we went to the Nylon Pool, which is in the middle of the sea and very shallow. Some of the grown-ups went scuba diving and one man came back with two starfish.

In the afternoon Keith and Yvonne took us to an old fort called Fort King George. They told us it was built by English soldiers in 1762. It had a cannon and an old jail house under a big tree. From the top of the fort we could see all of Tobago.

✳ Trinidad ✳

This morning we flew to Trinidad.
It only took an hour! When we
landed, Dad's friend Rolando
collected us and we went to stay
with Dad's parents in Morvant,
just outside Port of Spain. Grandad
has not one, but two gardens where
he grows lots of fruit and vegetables.

After lunch, Dad took us on a tour of Morvant. We went to see his old school, Morvant Anglican School, and while we were there some of his old school friends dropped in and we took a photo.

Dad couldn't get over the size of the school.

"When I went there, it was much smaller," he told me.

Today we went to a look-out high up on a hill where we could see the city below. A man was playing a guitar and making up calypsos about everyone. He made one up about Remi, my dad and me. He said I was going to be a cricketer like Brian Lara – one of Trinidad's cricketing heroes – and that Remi was going to be a nurse!

Then we went to Queens Park Savannah. It was like a giant roundabout surrounded by big old houses called The Magnificent Seven. One of them looked like a castle. There were lots of people buying sweets, out walking, playing football and, best of all, drinking fresh coconut water.

"This is definitely my favourite drink!" I told my dad.

Later we went to Rolando's friends' house and had fun in their pool.

Today we went to an art camp run by my mum's friend Auntie Tessa. Remi made a hut out of twigs and I painted a picture. We made some new friends, too.

When we got home we helped Grandad pick mangoes from the tree behind the house. I only had one, but Remi ate three!

Later, Rolando took us to see Port of Spain. We went to a promenade named after Brian Lara. It was noisy, full of cars, people playing music and selling food – like this man, who had coconuts for sale.

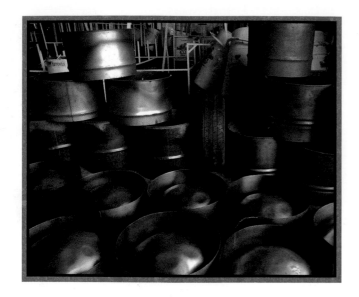

"Would you like to learn the steelpan?" asked my dad. "It's Trinidad and Tobago's national instrument – and it's the only musical instrument invented in the 20th century." Of course we said yes. So Grandad's friend Mr Grant took us to Solo Harmonites panyard, where they were making steelpans.

First, they take an old oil drum and cut it in half, then they bang the top of the drum to make a big dent, and finally someone else makes a pattern in the dent where the notes are going to be. It's a noisy job, and the man making them was wearing protective headphones.

Then they showed us how to play them, and we pretended we were in a real steelband. It was fun! I think I want to go on learning steelpans.

Today we went on a long drive to the other side of the island, to Pitch Lake. The guide said that there is only one other lake like it, in North America, and that when Sir Walter Raleigh came here from England over 300 years ago, he used the tar in the water to mend his ships.

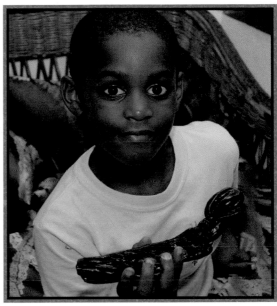

Pitch Lake is full of little puddles
of water with fish swimming in them.
We pushed a stick down into the lake
and when we pulled it out, it was
covered in tar.

As we were leaving, the guide gave
me a piece of 200-year-old wood.
When I get back, I'm going to take
it to school and show my teacher.

Today Mr Grant took us to the Asa Wright Nature Centre. It's up in the rainforest and full of lovely birds – toucans, yellow-bellies and hummingbirds.

We stood still and stayed very quiet on the verandah, and the hummingbirds flew in really close. We saw some beautiful flowers, too, like this water-lily.

In the afternoon we went to see Hanuman Murti and
the Temple in the Sea. Hanuman Murti is a tall statue of
Hanuman, the Hindu monkey god of the wind. It is the
tallest statue of Hanuman outside India. But you have to
be very careful what you say there, because if you make fun
of Hanuman, he'll blow you away!

The Temple in the Sea is a Hindu temple stretching out into the sea. It had flowers and Hindu gods inside and prayer flags outside to bring health and happiness. They were burning the body of a dead person, and we watched them throw his ashes into the sea afterwards.

Best of all, we went to the Caroni Swamp. We climbed into a boat just as the sun was going down and sailed along the river. We saw two boa constrictors, some tree crabs, caimans and lots and lots of scarlet ibis. When the sun set, the scarlet ibis flew home to the swamp to sleep.

Dad has often told us that Grandad was a soldier in World War II, so today I asked him about it. He showed us his album with photos from his time in the army. He told us about the battles he was in and the places he visited in Europe. He looked so young in the photos! He had medals, too.

Today we had a big party and everyone was invited!
Grandma got up early and went to buy fish from the
fishermen at a place called Small Boats.

"Look what I've bought," she said when she came back,
and showed us a fish almost as tall as she was. It weighed
nearly five kilos!

Whilst Grandma went home to get the fish ready, she sent Dad and me to market to buy things for the party.

When we got back, the guests were arriving, so we changed into our party clothes. Grandma and our neighbour Natalie were already cooking and Grandad was outside barbequing the chicken. He asked me to help him.

Then Grandma said "Food's ready!" so we went inside to eat. There was baked fish Creole, boiled plantain, white rice and avocado, but everyone said my barbequed chicken was the best part.

Before we left Trinidad to fly home, we had a family photo taken. I'm feeling a bit sad. I'm really going to miss everyone!

When he saw us off, Grandad asked Remi and me, "Would you like to live in Trinidad with Grandma and me one day?" and we said yes. We had lots of fun here, and I'm sure we'll be coming back one day soon.

MORE TITLES IN THE CHILDREN RETURN TO THEIR ROOTS SERIES
FROM FRANCES LINCOLN CHILDREN'S BOOKS

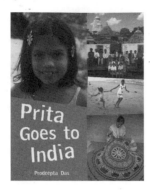

Prita Goes to India
Prodeepta Das

Seven-year-old Prita has come to India for the first time to visit her many relatives. She is fascinated by everything, from the Taj Mahal to the village shrines in Orissa; from delicious coconuts to market stalls filled with savoury snacks; but above all, by the way of life lived by her relatives. Some of it is like her life at home – but much of it is very different.

Shanyi Goes to China
Sungwan So

Arriving first in Hong Kong, Shanyi goes by train to Panyu in mainland China to see where her grandmother was born, visits her family's ancestral hall and is kept busy sightseeing, meeting relations, eating and shopping. From red bean pie to lunar calendars, from firecrackers to dragons, she learns all about China and returns home delighted with the land of her grandparents.

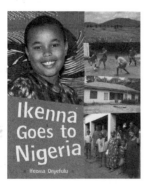

Ikenna Goes to Nigeria
Ifeoma Onyefulu

Visiting the country where his mother was born, Ikenna meets his cousins for the first time, travels from bustling modern Lagos to quiet Nkwelle, samples delicious Jellof Rice and sees the amazing Osun Festival. Ikenna enjoys so many exciting new experiences on the trip, but his most treasured memories to take back are of getting to know his extended family.

Frances Lincoln titles are available from all good bookshops.
You can also buy books and find out more about your favourite titles,
authors and illustrators on our website: www.franceslincoln.com

Oven Barbeque Chicken
cooked by Kamal

Serves 6

You'll need:

◆ 1 chicken cut into pieces

◆ 1 tsp salt

◆ ½ tsp black pepper

◆ 1 tsp minced garlic

◆ 2 tbsp green seasoning*

◆ A jar of barbeque sauce

✛ a grown-up on hand to help you.

*For the green seasoning you'll need:

◆ Spring onions

◆ Parsley

◆ Thyme

◆ Ginger

◆ Garlic cloves

To make the green seasoning:

Put all ingredients in a blender with a little water and blend until very smooth. Bottle, refrigerate and use within one week.

To make the barbeque chicken:

1. Season chicken with salt, black pepper, garlic and green seasoning.

2. Place chicken skin side up in a baking dish, cover with foil and bake for 35–40 minutes in a medium oven.

3. Remove from oven and drain off the juices.

4. Coat with barbeque sauce and return to oven.

5. Bake for 15 minutes more until the chicken is brown.

Glossary

Brian Lara: record-breaking cricketer and one of the greatest batsmen of all time, known as 'the Prince of Port-of-Spain'.

caiman: a small crocodile that lives in Central and South America.

calypso: a style of Afro-Caribbean music once used to spread news around Trinidad. Nowadays, calypso singers often make up instant words and music about other people, just for fun.

Hanuman Murti: an 85-foot statue of the Hindu monkey god Hanuman. Two-fifths of Trinidad and Tobago's population trace their ancestors back to India.

Hindu body-burning: the bodies of Hindus in India and some other places such as Trinidad are cremated or burnt outside on a wooden fire.

hummingbird: small birds which hover in mid-air by beating their wings very fast, making a humming noise. They are the only birds which can fly backwards.

Rasta: the Rastafari religion began in Jamaica and believes that Haile Selassie I, the former Emperor of Ethiopia, is the promised Messiah.

scarlet ibis: a special kind of crane found in tropical South America and Trinidad and Tobago. It is the national bird of Trinidad.

steelpans: a musical instrument made from oil-drums invented in Trinidad and Tobago. Steelbands are now extremely popular and play at carnivals, festivals and in churches worldwide.

toucan: brilliantly-coloured birds from the tropics known for their enormous, colourful beaks.

yellow-belly: a yellow-bellied bird also known as the Tropical Kingbird of Trinidad and Tobago.

✸ Index ✸